Showdown

Players Around the World

Lesley Ward

Publishing Credits

Rachelle Cracchiolo, M.S.Ed., *Publisher*
Conni Medina, M.A.Ed., *Managing Editor*
Nika Fabienke, Ed.D., *Series Developer*
June Kikuchi, *Content Director*
Michelle Jovin, M.A., *Assistant Editor*
Lee Aucoin, *Senior Graphic Designer*

Image Credits: Cover and pp.1, 22 Bossaball International; pp.4–5 Simon Balson/Alamy Stock Photo; pp.12–13 epa european pressphoto agency b.v./Alamy Stock Photo; pp.20–21 David Buzzard/Alamy Stock Photo; pp.22–23 Jaap Arriens/Alamy Stock Photo; all other images from iStock and/or Shutterstock.

Teacher Created Materials
5301 Oceanus Drive
Huntington Beach, CA 92649-1030
http://www.tcmpub.com

ISBN 978-1-4258-4967-2

Table of Contents

Who Is an Athlete?

A woman runs as fast as she can on a track. A man hits a baseball with a bat. A girl kicks a soccer ball through a goal. These people are athletes. Athletes play sports and compete.

Many athletes compete because they like to work out. Others like the feeling they get when they win. Some play sports because they like to work together with others. These people like to compete on teams. Whether you want to play on a team or alone, there is a sport for everyone!

Imani Lansiquot competes in the 2016 British Championships.

Preparation

Athletes practice the same moves over and over again. They do this to work on their **skills**. This is how they prepare for their next match. Soccer players run to build muscle. Skiers race down snowy mountains to find faster routes. Swimmers spend all day doing laps in a pool.

Beside each athlete is a coach. The coach's job is to help the athlete. The athlete's job is to listen to the coach. They depend on each other to succeed.

A skier practices to find faster routes.

Athletes also prepare by watching what they eat. They have to make sure to eat healthy. This means they eat a lot of fruits and vegetables and drink plenty of water. Eating healthy is one way they keep their bodies in shape.

Sleep is also important. Sleep helps fix tired muscles. Studies show that the more sleep you get, the more prepared you are to take on the day. So, snooze your way to success!

Drinking water is a great way to stay healthy.

Once the **preparation** is done, it is time to play! Many athletes play different sports. The skills they learn from one sport can help them play others.

Sometimes, people choose a sport based on the time of year. They might play baseball in the summer. But when it gets cold, they might switch to hockey. Other times, they might pick their sport based on where they live.

Ice hockey is a popular winter sport.

World Athlete Showdowns

Many sports are played around the world. Some sports are only played in certain places. But even the wildest sports share some **traits** with others.

Pole Climbers vs. Lumberjacks

A **unique** sport to play in India is mallakhamb (MALL-kham). The word *malla* means "wrestler." The word *khamb* means "pole."

These athletes climb up wooden poles. At the top, they do tricks for 90 seconds. To win, mallakhamb athletes must be strong and have great balance.

A Sport Without Sight

Mallakhamb is very popular with blind children. They must listen closely to their coaches. Then, they feel their way to the tops of the poles.

Across the world, in Canada, lumberjacks do not climb poles. They use poles to test their strength.

Lumberjacks race to see how fast they can saw big logs. They see how deep they can bury axes in tree trunks. They run on floating logs and try not to fall. Lumberjacks need strong arms and good balance to be the best.

This lumberjack uses his strength to saw through a thick log.

Showdown: Karate

To win a karate match, you have to be **flexible** and fast. Who would win a karate match—a mallakhamb athlete or a lumberjack? Why do you think so? What skills would help each athlete?

Sumo Wrestler vs. Netball Player

In Japan, two sumo wrestlers face each other in a round ring. They stamp their feet. Then, the **bout** begins. They push and shove each other.

To win, sumo wrestlers must force their **rivals** to the ground or push them out of the ring. Because strength is so important, sumo wrestlers must stay big and tough.

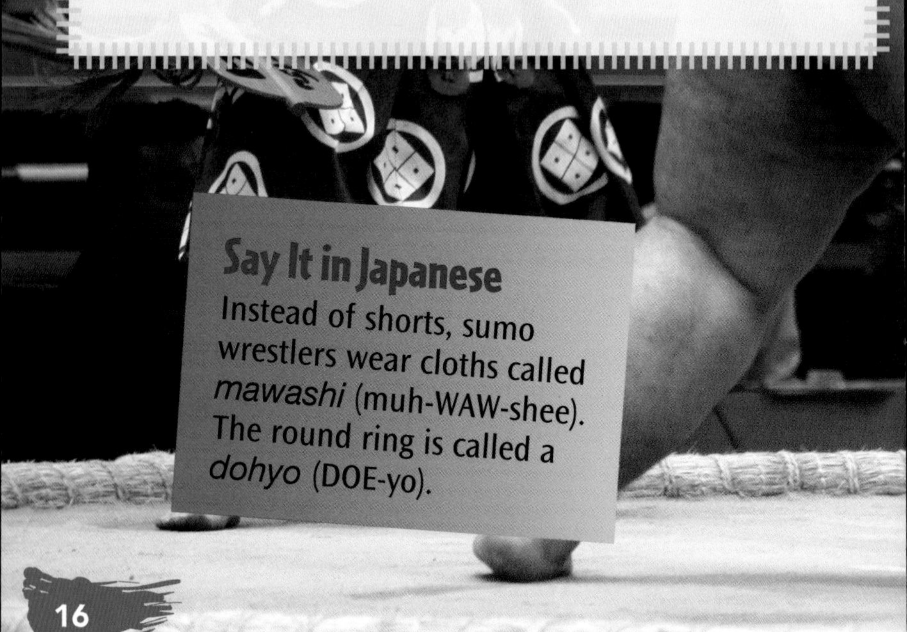

Say It in Japanese

Instead of shorts, sumo wrestlers wear cloths called *mawashi* (muh-WAW-shee). The round ring is called a *dohyo* (DOE-yo).

Sumo wrestlers compete in Tokyo, Japan.

In Australia, speed not strength, is key for netball. This fast-paced sport may look like a game of basketball. But the rules are not the same.

In netball, players may not run with the ball. Instead, they must throw it from where they stand. And there are no backboards on these hoops. To win, netball players must be able to run and change direction quickly.

Showdown: Dodgeball

To win in dodgeball, you must be able to dart away from the ball. Who would win a dodgeball game—a sumo wrestler or a netball player? Why do you think so? What skills would help each athlete?

Roller Derby Skater vs. Bossaball Player

In the United States, roller derby skaters speed around a track. The fastest team wins.

"Jammers" score points for being the fastest. "Blockers" try to slow them down or stop them from passing. They knock each other out of the way. There are many crashes and falls! Brave skaters must be able to skate fast to win roller derby.

This blocker tries to keep a jammer from scoring by knocking her off the track.

Wild Names

Roller derby skaters call themselves clever names. You might cheer for a jammer called “Fire Kracker.” “Ima Zombie” might push a rival off the track. “Kandy Barr” might block a lot of points!

In Spain, brave athletes have their own sport—bossaball. It is a mix of many sports. You might see things that look like they came straight out of a volleyball or soccer match.

But that is not the only thing that makes this sport unique. It is also played on trampolines!

Players flip and bounce high in the air. They try to hit balls over nets to score. The best bossaball players are strong and flexible.

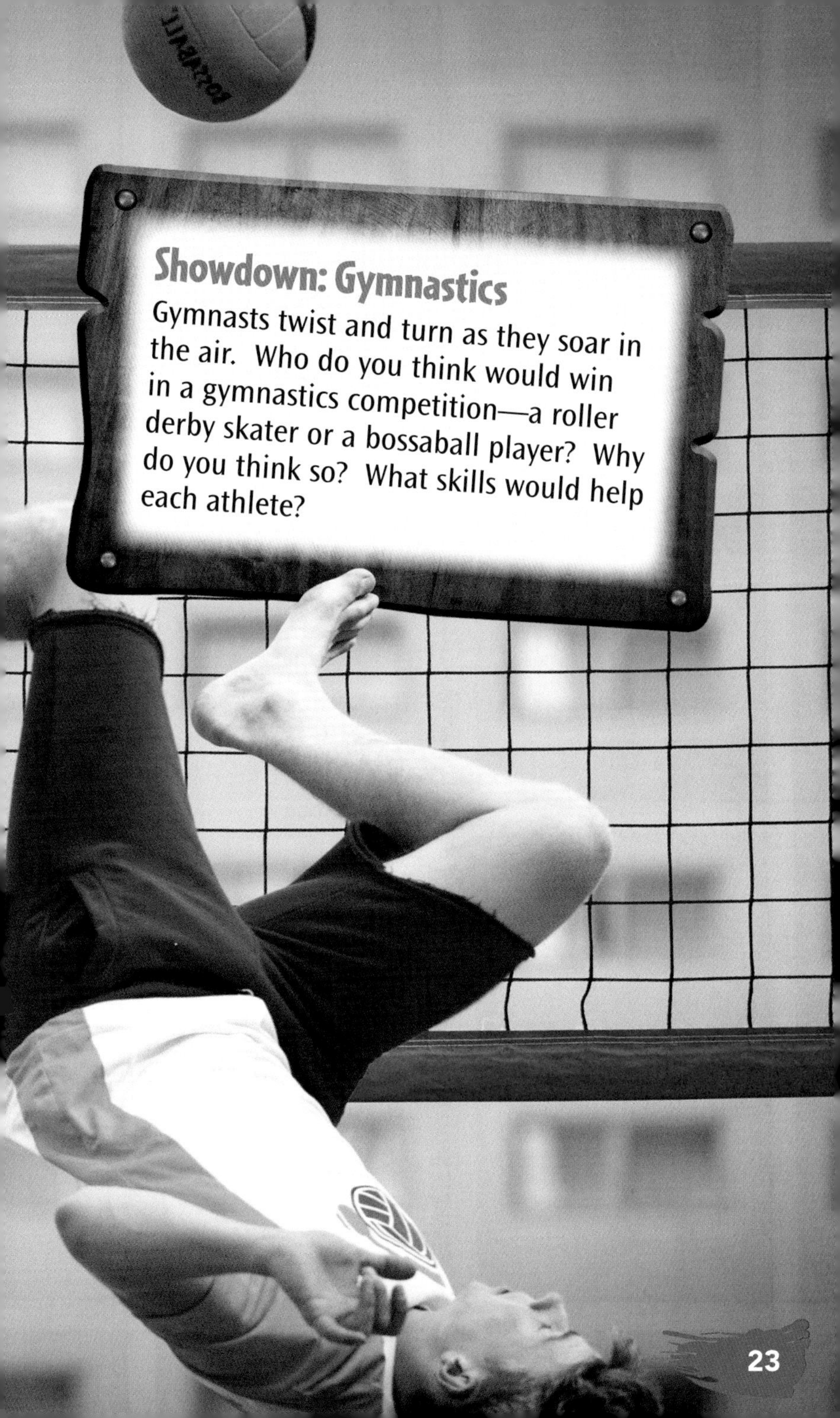

Showdown: Gymnastics

Gymnasts twist and turn as they soar in the air. Who do you think would win in a gymnastics competition—a roller derby skater or a bossaball player? Why do you think so? What skills would help each athlete?

Rules of the Game

Rules explain how to play the game and what it takes to win. Rules make a game run smoothly. Because of rules, all players are treated fairly.

Rules are also important to winning. If you do not follow the rules, you might lose points or have to sit out for part of the game. You might even be removed from the game!

A football player sits out during a game.

In soccer, if you do not follow the rules, the referee may give you a red card.

Find Your Sport

You have learned about some unique sports. You do not have to travel around the world to try them! Bounce on a trampoline to practice your bossaball skills. Shoot some hoops to see if you like netball. Skate around your neighborhood to train for roller derby. Or make up your own sport!

Practice the skills you will need to succeed. Sometimes you will win, and sometimes you will lose. But you will always have fun.

Good Game!

You can say "good game" in many languages. In Japan, it is "Yoi gēmu" (YOY GHEY-mu). In Spain, it is "Buen juego" (BWEN HWAY-go). An Australian athlete might say, "Well played, mate!"

This tennis player practices to be the best.

Glossary

bout—a contest or match

flexible—capable of bending different ways

preparation—steps that are taken to get ready for something

rivals—people who try to beat others at something

skills—abilities that come from training and practice

traits—qualities that people or things in groups share

unique—special or unusual